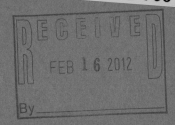

KNIGHT
SURVIVAL
GUIDE

Anna Claybourne

Crabtree Publishing Company

www.crabtreebooks.com

Author: Anna Claybourne
Editors: Kathy Middleton
Crystal Sikkens
Project coordinator: Kathy Middleton
Production coordinator: Ken Wright
Prepress technicians: Ken Wright
Margaret Amy Salter

Picture Credits:
Corbis: Lebrecht Music & Arts: page 19
Dreamstime: Aleksander Lorenz: page 14; Thomas
Ramage: pages 1, 15
Shutterstock: cover; Hintau Aliaksei: page 18; Bortel
Pavel: page 20; CSLD: page 17; Demid: page 8; Dibrova:
pages 3, 12; Sergii Figurnyi: page 9; Abramova Kseniya:
page 6; Steve Mann: page 13; Razumovskaya Marina
Nikolaevna: page 7; PetrMalyshev: page 21; Nicholas
Piccillo: page 4; Puchan: page 5; Raulin: page 10; St.
Nick: page 11; Johannes Wiebel: page 16

Every effort has been made to trace copyright holders and to obtain their
permission for use of copyright material. The authors and publishers
would be pleased to rectify any error or omission in future editions.
All the Internet addresses given in this book were correct at the time of
going to press. The author and publishers regret any inconvenience
caused if addresses have changed or sites have ceased to exist, but can
accept no responsibility for any such changes.

Library and Archives Canada Cataloguing in Publication

Claybourne, Anna
Knight survival guide / Anna Claybourne.

(Crabtree connections)
Includes index.
ISBN 978-0-7787-7855-4 (bound).--ISBN 978-0-7787-7877-6 (pbk.)

1. Knights and knighthood--Europe--History--Juvenile
literature. 2. Civilization, Medieval--Juvenile literature.
I. Title. II. Series: Crabtree connections

CR4513.C54 2011   j940.1   C2011-900607-3

Library of Congress Cataloging-in-Publication Data

Claybourne, Anna.
Knight survival guide / Anna Claybourne.
p. cm. -- (Crabtree connections)
Includes index.
ISBN 978-0-7787-7877-6 (pbk. : alk. paper) -- ISBN 978-0-7787-7855-4
(reinforced library binding : alk. paper)
1. Knights and knighthood--Europe--History--Juvenile literature.
2. Civilization, Medieval--Juvenile literature. 3. Chivalry--Europe--
History--Juvenile literature. I. Title. II. Series.

CR4513.C55 2012
940.1--dc22
                                                  2011001346

Crabtree Publishing Company

www.crabtreebooks.com   1-800-387-7650

Printed in the U.S.A./072011/WO20110114

Published in Canada
Crabtree Publishing
616 Welland Ave.
St. Catharines, Ontario
L2M 5V6

Published in the United States
Crabtree Publishing
PMB 59051
350 Fifth Avenue, 59th Floor
New York, New York 10118

Contents

Tough Stuff

Being a knight is GREAT! You can fight in battles and go on big adventures—you even have your own horse!

Are you tough enough?

Being a knight is fun, but it's not an easy ride. You must be strong, tough, and very brave.

 Knights wear a lot of **armor**.

armor

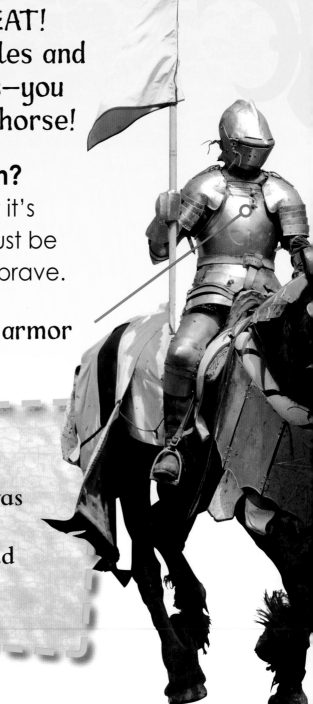

Heavy armor

A knight's armor was very heavy, so the horses they rode had to be super-strong.

A knight's job

Knights were soldiers who rode horses and went into battle for their king or **lord**.

lord

In Training

You will start training to be a knight when you are seven years old. You will be sent to work in a lord's castle as a **page**.

A tough job

Life as a page is hard work. You must:

1. Take messages for your lord.
2. Learn good manners.
3. Tidy up after your lord and keep his rooms clean.

You will learn how to ride and fight.

Becoming a squire

At 14 years old, a page became a squire. Then he helped a knight with his horse and armor.

squire

Into battle

Squires went into battle with their knight and fought by his side.

Fighting Talk

A knight's main job is to fight, so you will need top sword skills to beat your enemy. You will also need to train for battle.

Take that!

You will fight with a heavy sword. If you *can* lift it:

1. Swing it from side to side.
2. Use it to slash and bash!

Sticky head

If a knight hurt his head, his hair was shaved off, and his head was covered in oil, honey, and roses.

Pick a weapon

Knights used a lot of weapons, including a **battle-axe**, **pike** or **lance**, and a **mace**.

battle-axe

Hold your sword with two hands.

In Battle

You will need to be brave in battle. Charge in on horseback with your fellow knights and carry pikes to stab your **enemies**.

Cover up

Your enemies are soldiers with spears, bows, and arrows. To stay safe:

1. Wear armor.
2. Carry a shield.

No running away now!

Raining arrows

Knights fired rows of arrows at their enemies.

Hard head

Knights wore thick helmets to stop their heads and faces from being cut in battle.

shield

Getting Caught

Knights' fights are dangerous and it is very hard to **survive**. Even if you do manage to stay alive, you might still be caught by your enemies.

Knight for sale

Your enemies will give you back to your lord—for a **ransom**. If your lord has enough cash (and if he likes you enough), you should be freed.

Pricey knights

To win back a really great knight, a lord would pay a large ransom of gold or land.

Fair fights

Captured knights were kept in a castle, but they were treated fairly.

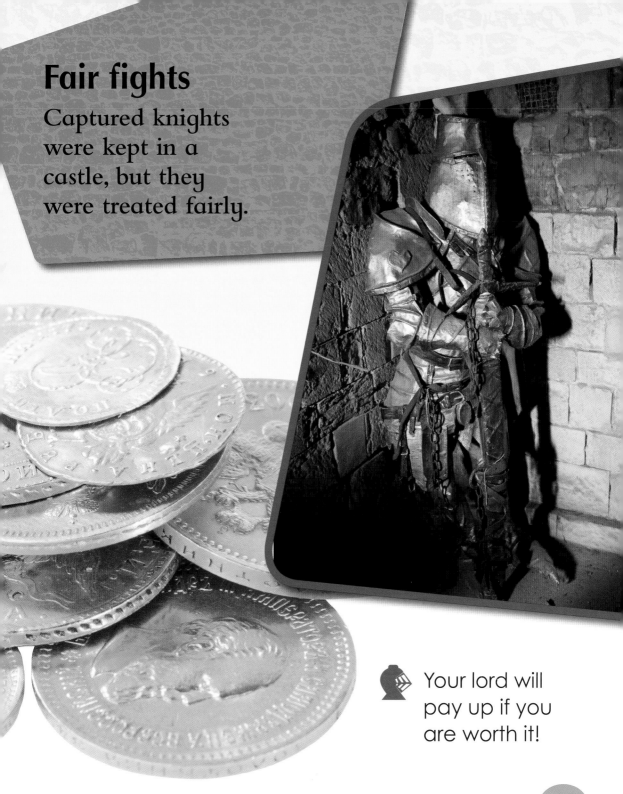

Your lord will pay up if you are worth it!

Showing Off

When there are no real battles, take part in a **tournament**. This is a fighting competition in which you can show off your skills.

Charge!

To **joust** you must:

1. Ride toward your enemy at top speed.
2. Try to hit him with your lance.

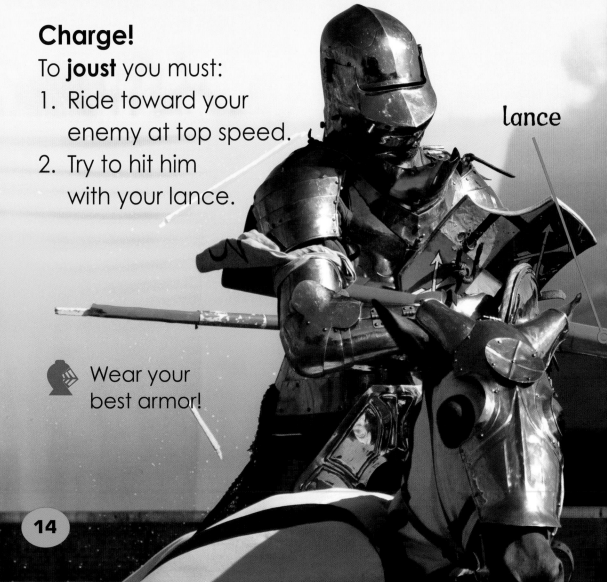

lance

Wear your best armor!

The winners

Knights who won a joust were given a prize. They were usually given money.

For the ladies

Knights sometimes fought to impress a lady.

Knight Rules

A good knight must be very polite to ladies. Always **bow** and kneel to a lady and never, ever swear at her!

Your special lady

You can even fight for a lady. In any fight, make sure you wear her family colors or **coat of arms**.

 Knights put their own coat of arms on their shields.

Take care

Knights were expected to **defend** and **protect** women.

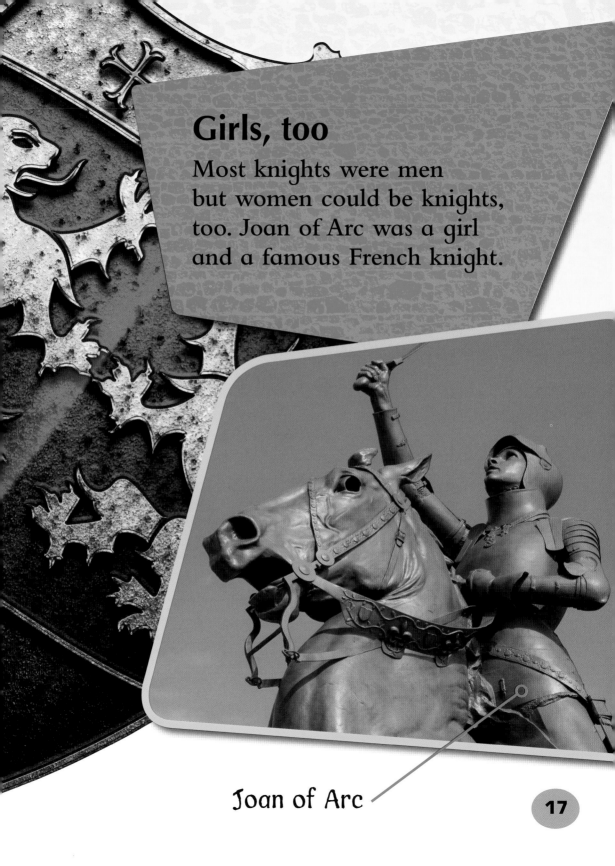

Girls, too

Most knights were men
but women could be knights,
too. Joan of Arc was a girl
and a famous French knight.

Joan of Arc

At Parties

As a knight, you will go to a lot of **feasts**. Talk to the ladies, play board games, and don't forget your manners.

It's my party!

If you have your own castle, you can throw feasts yourself. Use them to make friends with important people, such as kings.

Let's dance

Knights had to learn the latest dances to show off at parties.

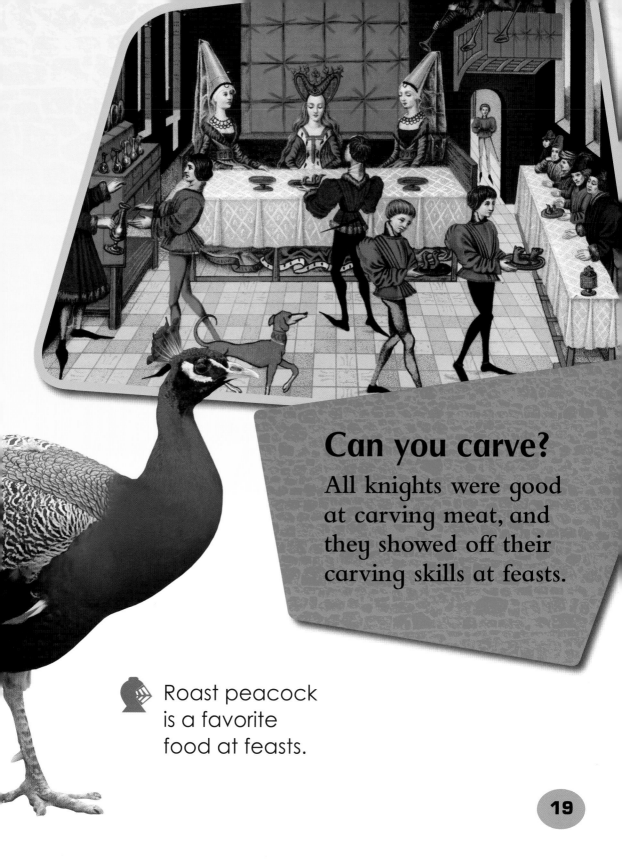

Can you carve?

All knights were good at carving meat, and they showed off their carving skills at feasts.

Roast peacock is a favorite food at feasts.

On a Mission

Your king or lord might test you by sending you on a quest, or mission. You might have to catch an enemy or save a prisoner in a castle.

Top quests

If you are really lucky you might get to find treasure or rescue a princess from a tower. And all knights want to fight a dragon, of course!

Cup of magic

Some knights went on a great adventure to find a magical cup called the Holy Grail.

Famous knights

In many famous stories, knights rescued princesses or ladies who had been taken prisoner by a wicked lord or king.

Dragons are terrifying beasts!

21

Glossary

armor A metal suit worn to protect the body in battle

battle-axe A short, heavy axe

bow To bend over at the waist

coat of arms A special family design

defend To stop something or someone from being hurt

enemies People who want to harm another person or other people

feasts Parties where people eat a lot of food

joust When two knights on horses charge at each other with lances

lance A long, wooden pole

lord An important man who had a large house or castle

mace A long club with a heavy weight on the end

page A boy training to be a knight

pike A long-handled spear

protect To take care of something or someone

ransom Money paid to set someone free

survive To stay alive

tournament A contest where knights test their skills

Further Reading

Web Sites

Learn how to make your own armor at:
**www.activityvillage.co.uk/knight_crafts_
  and_costume.htm**

Have fun coloring some knights, princesses, kings, and castles at:
**www.kids-n-fun.com/coloringpages/kleurplaat_
  Knights_88.aspx**

Try an online joust at:
www.tudorbritain.org/joust/index.asp

Books

The Life of a Knight (Medieval World) by Kay Eastwood, Crabtree Publishing (2004).

Joan of Arc by Diane Stanley, Harpercollins (2002).

Knights (Horrible Histories Handbooks) by Terry Deary, Scholastic (2006).

A Day in the Life of a Knight by Andrea Hopkins, PowerKids Press (2007).

Index